A WINNING SKILLS BOOK

You Can Be A Winner!

Joy Berry

Illustrated by Bartholomew

Joy Berry Enterprises

Copyright © Joy Berry, 2022
Originally Published 2013

All rights are reserved.

No part of this book can be duplicated or used without the prior written permission of the copyright owner, except for the use of brief quotations from the book.

For inquiries or permission requests contact the publisher.

Published by Joy Berry Enterprises
www.joyberryenterprises.com

Joy Berry Enterprises

You can be a winner by
- understanding winning.
- establishing realistic goals.
- developing a plan of action, and
- following six rules that winners follow.

You need to achieve something in order to be healthy.

In order to be happy you need to achieve something.

There will always be goals that you **need** to achieve.

There will always be goals that you **want** to achieve.

UNDERSTANDING WINNING

Whenever you achieve something **you win!**

Some of your achievements may require you to make a special effort. The more effort you make, the more you will enjoy winning.

In order to be a winner, you need to **set yourself up to win!**

First you must **decide what you want to achieve.** In other words, you need to establish a goal.

ESTABLISHING REALISTIC GOALS

Be realistic when you are deciding on a goal.

Find out exactly what it will take to achieve the goal. Research the subject.
- Read.
- Observe.
- Experiment.
- Talk to other people.

ESTABLISHING REALISTIC GOALS

Think about whether you are physically able to achieve the goal.

Consider your
- age,
- body size,
- body shape,
- physical coordination, and
- physical abilities.

ESTABLISHING REALISTIC GOALS

Think about whether you are mentally able to achieve the goal.

Consider your
- interests and
- mental abilities.

ESTABLISHING REALISTIC GOALS

Think about whether **conditions** are right for you to achieve the goal.

Consider **where** you live, work, and go to school. Can your environment provide what you need achieve the goal?

Consider the **people** around you. Are there people around you who can and will help you achieve the goal?

ESTABLISHING REALISTIC GOALS

Consider the **resources** that are available to you. Do you have access to the things you will need to achieve the goal?

Consider the **time** involved. Do you have enough time to achieve the goal?

DEVELOPING A PLAN OF ACTION

Once you have decided on a goal, you need to **develop a plan of action.**

Do this by making a list of the tasks you need to do to achieve your goal.

Next, organize your list. Put the tasks in the order in which they must be completed.

Once you have set yourself up to win, you are ready to be a winner.

Winners follow six rules.

Rule #1: Winners think good thoughts.

They think positive thoughts about themselves and what they are doing.

Your mind is extremely powerful. It controls everything you do. If it tells you to succeed, you will most likely succeed. If it tells you to fail, you will most likely fail. Therefore, it is important for you to think positive thoughts and avoid thinking negative ones.

Rule #2: Winners focus on the goal.

They think about the positive outcome of their efforts rather than the work and risk involved.

If you think about all you need to do to win, you may feel overwhelmed and want to give up. If you think about losing, you may become discouraged and stop trying. But if you think about winning, you will be inspired. Everything you do will be less difficult and you will want to keep trying. This is why you need to focus on your goal.

Rule #3: Winners keep their word.

They do what they say they will do. They keep the promises they make to others and, more important, they keep the promises they make to themselves.

If you want to keep your word, you must not **procrastinate** or **escape**. You must not put off what needs to be done or try to avoid doing a task by doing something else. Procrastinating or escaping can prevent you from keeping your word. When you have promised to do something it is important to do it as soon as you can.

Rule #4: Winners take advantage of competition.

They use competition in a positive rather than a negative way.

The Positive Side of Competition

Competition can help you learn what you should and should not do. It enables you to observe other people. As you see them making mistakes, you can learn to avoid those mistakes. As you see them succeeding, you can learn what you need to do to succeed.

Competition can make you want to **improve**. It allows you to compare your efforts with the efforts of others. Seeing what other people achieve can encourage you to do as well or even better than they have done.

Competition can encourage you to try because it shows you what is possible. When you see someone do something, you learn that it can be done. This might make you more willing to try something. Being willing to try is important because you cannot win if you do not try.

The Negative Side of Competition

Competition can **distract** you. If you want to win, you must pay attention to what you are doing. You cannot do this if you are spending your time and energy watching other people. It is important for you to concentrate on *your* efforts, rather than on the efforts of others.

Competition can **discourage** you. Focusing on the accomplishments of other people may cause you to feel inferior. You may begin to think that you cannot do as well as they. You may become discouraged and stop trying. If you want to win, you must remain confident and hopeful so that you do not give up.

Competition can **limit** you. Focusing on the achievements of others may cause you to think that what they are doing is all that can be done. But you may have the potential to do something that no other person has thought of doing. This is why you must not allow the accomplishments of others to limit you. Instead, you need to be creative and decide for yourself what you are going to do.

Competition can be used in a negative way to **dominate and control others.** Some people compete to prove they are better than others. They want to be considered better so they can dominate and control others. They want to have their way all the time. This is unfair and can cause many problems. Therefore, you must not compete to dominate and control others.

Rule #5: Winners take advantage of setbacks.

A setback happens when something goes wrong. A winner turns setbacks into something positive.

When things go wrong, you are usually forced to stop what you are doing for a while. **You can use this time to your advantage.** Think about what you are doing. Re-evaluate your efforts. You may discover that it is better to do things differently.

If you find that you need to do things differently, **revise your plan.** Your new plan will most likely be better than your old one.

Having a new plan can help you try harder and increase your chances of winning.

It is important that you not focus on setbacks. It is also important that you **not become discouraged and give up.** It is better for you to focus your time and energy making your new plan work.

It may help to remember that setbacks are bound to occur because people cannot always control everything that happens to them. Anyone who tries to accomplish things usually has one or more setbacks.

Rule #6: Winners take advantage of failure.

A winner turns failure into something positive.

Failure can give you an opportunity to learn what you should and should not do. If you fail because you did something wrong, you can learn to avoid doing the same thing again. If you fail because you neglected to do something, you can learn to do it the next time.

You can learn from failure if you respond to it appropriately. You must not focus on the failure. Focusing on the failure will only make you feel bad. Instead, you must focus on the lessons to be learned.

You must not be impatient with yourself when you fail. Being impatient with yourself will only make you feel as though you cannot do anything right. When you feel this way, you are not able to do your best. If you do not do your best, you may not be able to win.

It may help to remember that everyone fails at one time or another. Failure seems to be something that every winner must go through to win.

CONCLUSION

You can be a winner if you
- decide on a realistic goal,
- develop a plan of action,
- think good thoughts,
- focus on your goal,
- keep your word,
- take advantage of competition,
- take advantage of setbacks, and
- take advantage of failure.

www.ingramcontent.com/pod-product-compliance
Lightning Source LLC
Chambersburg PA
CBHW081408070526
44583CB00020B/2729